By Vanda North with Tony Buzan

Get Ahead

Mind Map® your way to success

and for his devotion and energy towards achieving his goal of having the world's population Mentally Literate.

Now, you are part of making this dream come true. It is my joy to share Mind Mapping with you. I hope it helps you as much as it helps me.

INTRODUCTION
by VANDA NORTH

In 1978 I read a book called „Use Your Head". I felt like a person receiving oxygen after almost suffocating. The key process, Mind Maps, created by Tony Buzan, was exactely what I had been searching for.

My search was for an easily useable, widely applicable process that would allow the vast potential of the brain to be developed; to make Learning to Learn as easy and natural for everyone as it is for the very young; for universal teaching of whole brain process; to reduce the pain of being labled as „learning disabled" and enhance the thinking capabilities of all learners regardless of age or abilitiy.

Amazingly; Mind Maps® answered all these needs.

„Get Ahead" is dedicated to Tony Buzan to thank him for creating this brillant, simple yet deeply profound process

FORWORD
by TONY BUZAN

From „Use Your Head"
to „Get Ahead"!

When I was 7 years old I began to wonder what made me and my class mates in school either „tick" or „not tick". Sometimes those of us who knew less about a subject seemed to do better on tests and exams than others who knew more. At other times the reverse was true: we who knew more did worse than those whom we had actually taught. For years, like a little terrier, I „worried" at these questions.

Eventually my university work and practical experience led me to the conclusion that the prime reason for all these differences was the approprate or inappropriate use of the massive potential of our young brains.

The result of years of questioning, research and work was the creation of Mind Maps, and the publication in 1974 of my book „Use Your Head".

My dream at this time was that as many people as possible should know, what an amazing organ the brain was, and that they should be able to learn how to use the enormous abilities they all had.

This dream has been coming increasingly true, thanks in large part to Vanda North's extraordinary dedication, effort, and profound knowledge of the subject.

Vanda has become the world's leading exponent in the teaching worldwide, of Mind Maps and its related skills and applications.

With „Get Ahead" the move towards a Mentally Literate world, will itself Get Ahead!

Get Ahead

To read this Mind Map® start in the centre and
follow the branches out, beginning at 1 o'clock.

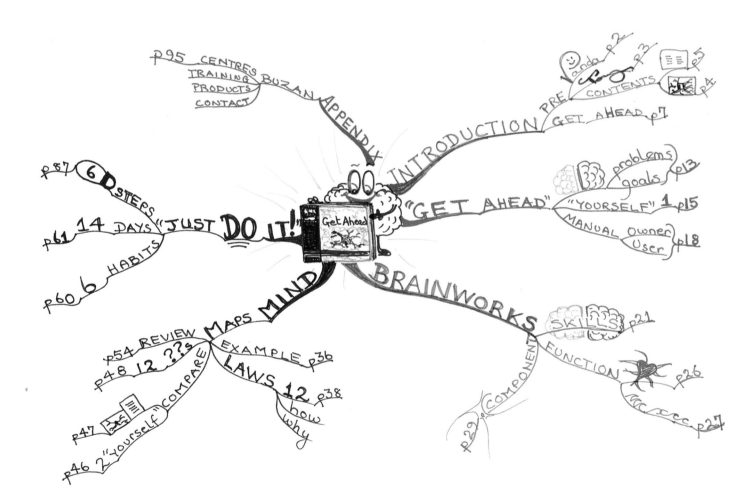

p95 CENTRES
TRAINING BUZAN APPENDIX
PRODUCTS
CONTACT

panda p2
p3
p5
PRE CONTENTS p4
INTRODUCTION GET AHEAD p7

problems p13
goals
"YOURSELF" 1 p15
MANUAL owner p18
User

p87 6 STEPS
p61 14 DAYS "JUST DO IT!"
p60 6 HABITS

"GET AHEAD"

BRAINWORKS
SKILLS p21
COMPONENT FUNCTION p26
p29 p27

p54 REVIEW MAPS MIND
p48 12 ??s EXAMPLE p36
COMPARE LAWS 12 p38
p47 how
p46 2 "yourself" why

We'll show you how to:
LEARN how you LEARN + THINK
with MIND MAPS®

Words from Vanda and Tony	p2
Mind Map of Contents	p4
Table of Contents	p5
Introduction	**p6**
Get Ahead	**p9**
Brains-Problems & Goals	p13
Yourself 1	p15
Taught How?!	p16
Owner's & User's Manual	p18
BrainWorks	**p19**
Brain Skills	p21
Brain Functions	p25
Brain Components	p29
Mind Maps®	**p33**
How to Read a Mind Map	p36
12 Laws of Mind Maps	p38
Yourself 2	p46
Comparison	p47
12 Questions Asked	p48
Review of the Laws	p54
Just Do It! Programme	**p57**
Two Week Programme	p58
6 Steps to a New Habit	p60
Day 1 – Expanding	p61
Day 2 – Unscrambling	p63
Note Making	p64
Day 3 – Writing	p65
Day 4 – Converting	p66
Day 5 – Speaking	p68
Day 6 – Playing	p69
Day 7 – Exploring	p70
Note Taking	p71
Day 8 – A Book	p73
Day 9 – A Show	p76
Thinking Skills	p77
Day 10 – Deciding	p79
Day 11 – BrainBlooming	p81
Day 12 – Planning	p83
Day 13 – Rewarding	p85
Day 14 – Celebrating	p86
6 Steps to RadiantThinking	p87
36 Problems Solved!	p90
Appendix	
Buzan Centre Training & Products	p95

Introduction

GET
A
HEAD

Aha...
just as
we
suspected...

So...
here is your
owner's & user's manual
for it...

you
already
have
one!

HIGHLIGHTS:

- Develop your natural genius
- Discover your brain's problems and goals
- Get your brain's „owner's & user's manual"

Get Ahead!

Turn the pages of this book to know how to

LEARN
HOW
YOUR HEAD
LEARNS
& THINKS

If you watch babies „LEARNING" they use:

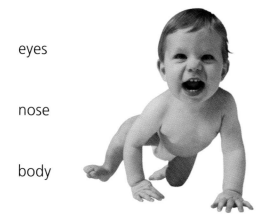

eyes　　　　　　　　　　ears

nose　　　　　　　　　　mouth

body　　　　　　　　　　hands

their whole brain and ALL of their Senses

Every baby and grown-up and „Great and Clever Brain" learns the same way

creating a

vibrant

AMAZING,

Unique

HUMAN BEING

This book is full of practical hints on learning how to learn, and amazing information on your brain.

This is a little book, introducing a simple technique that frees your mind's marvellous abilities and re-develops your

NATURAL
CHILDHOOD
GENIUS

You are just *a few*
hours from beginning to
realise **YOUR** true genius...

YES! There is *more* in there – just as you have dreamed!

So, do you wonder why it doesn't seem to work very well sometimes?

The first *UGO on the next page, lets you explore how you feel about problems with or goals for your brain and mental abilities.

It provides a benchmark for the start of our journey.

*UGO Definition

You have a go!
So that you may participate with us in GET AHEAD, we'll ask or tell you something, then YOU GO!

List all the **problems** with your BRAIN below:

for example: Mind wandering

List all the **goals** for your BRAIN below:

for example: Read faster

Problems to be solved! Goals to be achieved!

These are some of the more frequently mentioned problems, gathered from over 100,000 people around the world

REMEMBERING
CONCENTRATING
PLANNING
MANAGING TIME
MANAGING INFORMATION
MANAGING PROJECTS
MANAGING KNOWLEDGE
MOTIVATING
PUBLIC SPEAKING
PROBLEM ANALYSING
PROBLEM SOLVING
ORGANISING THOUGHTS
DELEGATING

EXPRESSING
RECALLING FACTS
COMMUNICATING EFFECTIVELY
PRIORITISING
STUDYING
DECISION MAKING
STARTING THINKING
STOPPING THINKING
LOGICAL THINKING
CREATIVE THINKING
BRAIN-STORMING
PREPARING
EXAM TAKING
FINISHING

and.... PROCRASTINATING!

For comparison later, spend the next five minutes writing as much as you can about yourself (past, present or future) on this page.

*YOUR*self
description 1

If you had any problems with this activity, please write them here. For example: mind went blank.

In all fairness, *have you ever been told* how to make it

Sometimes you can feel as if you've been given a 'lemon' of a brain BUT **have you ever been taught how to:**

	Y	N

- **Organise your thoughts** in a way that is compatible with how your brain works?
- **Let your thoughts flow**, so you can see how much you know on any subject?
- **Prepare a speech** of any length on one piece of paper and in 1/4 of your usual time?
- **Gather a lot of information** on one page, so you may see the relationship of any piece of information to any other?
- **Improve your memory** by using the natural processes of your brain?
- **Make Learning, Thinking & Studying FUN?!?**
- Weigh many opinions and **make a decision?**

You will have been taught all of these by the time you reach page 89.

This **OWNER'S & USER'S MANUAL** shows you one easy (yet wonderfully profound) PROCESS that can assist you with:

- concentrating
- memorising
- logical thinking
- decision making
- writing: reports/letters
- brain-storming
- creative thinking
- planning
- prioritising
- managing time
- starting to think
- motivating
- public speaking
- problem solving
- communicating

This process is the thought organiser
Mind Maps®
(Originated by Tony Buzan in 1971)

A MIND MAP can help you with many of those problems and goals BECAUSE it is a **REFLECTION** of the way your brain works

As the name implies, it is like a MAP of your MIND.

Just as a road map gives you an overview of a large area, a Mind Map can help you to:

- plan
- make choices
- know where you're going
- gather data
- be efficient
- think
- solve problems
- see the whole picture, and
- see the details
- enjoy...

17

**Your Owner's & User's Manual, „Get Ahead"
will show you how to Mind Map, enabling
you to Learn how you Learn and Think in a
BrainFriendly way. This will make many
everyday tasks much easier, (and enjoyable!)**

BIT DARK IN HERE　　　　BEGINNING TO LEARN　　　　USING YOUR HEAD TO GET AHEAD

HIGHLIGHTS:

- Your 12 brain skills
- Your associative „bloom" & „flow"
- Your brain cells

BRAINWORKS

We don't often give *Thought* to how we think.

We are in the middle of our thoughts, like the fish in water.

So let's float above our brains, and LOOK at their:

SKILLS

        FUNCTIONS &

                COMPONENTS

Brain *Skills*

Seen from above your brain's cortex (outer part) is divided into TWO halves the LEFT & RIGHT.

These halves have dominant and compatible cerebral (brain) skills which communicate, back and forth, almost like two people! You use ALL these skills every day of your life.

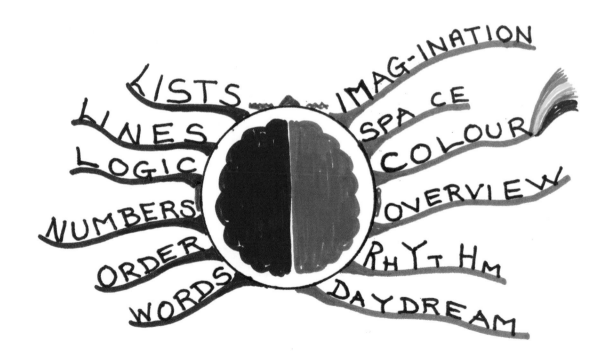

These *Skills* support and enrich, watch over and assist each other.

Based on these left and right brainskills consider:

1 What skills does a baby use to learn?

_____

_____

2 What skills are used and recognised in school?

_____

_____

3 What skills are used for note taking and note making?

_____

_____

4 What skills are thought to be Academic, Intellectual & Business like?

_____

_____

5 What skills are thought to be Creative Artistic?

_____

_____

6 What skills do the people we call "Great" use?

_____

_____

What conclusion can you make?

_____

_____

If you use numbers, logic, words, lines, lists, order, space, day dreams, imagination, rhythm, overview and colour

TOGETHER

YOUR WHOLE BRAIN WILL WORK BETTER FOR YOU!

So far our school, culture & work emphasises the skills of the **left** context.

However, as a child you **naturally** used the **left and right** together.
Our research on the „Great Brains" discovered that they also used the right and left together.

How can you integrate the RIGHT skills into your life, study & work?

RIGHT SKILLS	LIFE	STUDY	WORK
Imagination			
Space			
Colour			
Overview			
Rhythm			
Daydream			

You will increase your efficiency AND your enjoyment.

Brain
Functions

All those skills operate best when your brain is allowed to function the way it was designed.

So **ANY:**

**WORD,
SMELL,
SYMBOL,
IMAGE,
NUMBER,
TASTE,
SOUND,
TOUCH and
EMOTION**

Your brain functions by

ASSOCIATING
LINKING
CONNECTING

This way any information will be registered by your brain.

CONNECTS and **ASSOCIATES** with lots and lots of others…

based on **YOUR life experiences** in **YOUR unique way.**

25

Association
the 'Bloom'

To show you how amazingly associative and unique your brain is do some „Blooming" associations. ON EACH LINE place one word, (see example) which IMMEDIATELY pops into your mind when you think of the word LOVE.

EXAMPLE

For more FUN: Have 2 or more friends or family members do this activity… Keep your words secret until they have finished writing.Then exchange and compare.

HOW MANY OF THE 10 WORDS ARE EXACTLY THE SAME? SURPRISED?!

Association
the 'Flow'

These are our „flowing" associations from the
word **„water"**:

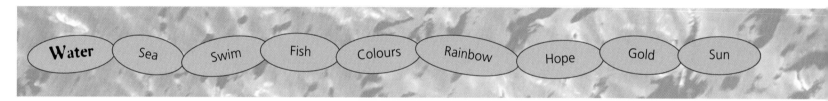

Water — Sea — Swim — Fish — Colours — Rainbow — Hope — Gold — Sun

Now try your own
associations:

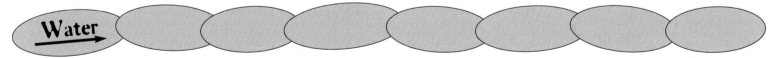

Water →

ASSOCIATING LINKING CONNECTING

is how
your brain functions,
tying all
your data together.

And your brain's
ability to associate
is infinite.

This reveals a **SURPRISE SECRET** that will improve your memory!

 Included in your **OWNER'S & USER'S MANUAL** is information that will help you to make remembering and recalling easy
(**Retaining –**
is putting it IN your head
Recalling –
is getting it back OUT again)

RETAINING:

Associative HOOKS (the „Bloom")
Put many „hooks" on the data you wish to remember by:
- Using all your senses
- Using strong key words or images

The more „hooks" you have, the richer the initial memory, and therefore it is easier to recall.

RECALLING:

Associative LINKS (the „Flow")
ASSOCIATE one new piece of data with relevant things you know. For review – travel along this linking memory chain to make RECALL easier.

And now,

Your *Brain's* Components
(the building blocks of your brain)

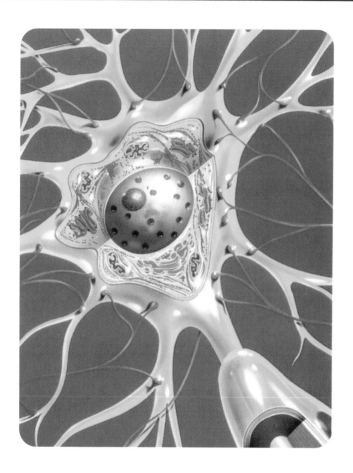

A question MANY people ask us is ...

„HOW BIG is my brain?"

**Do you feel YOURS too small
or WORSE,
not even there at all?**

Well, the answer is that

YOUR BRAIN is „BIGGER" THAN YOU THINK!

This is a **BRAIN CELL.** It is the basic building block of your brain. And it takes a very big number...

1,000,000,000,000

or a million million to fill your brain.
Further, they are all wrapped in an enourmous, intricate cuddle.

What actually happens
when *you learn*
something new?

When you have a thought, an idea or learn
something new these **brain cells interlink**
passing the information down the branch of one
cell across and over to another, like so:

This creates a pattern known medically as a
„memory trace", or more often called a
habit, learning or memory.

This gives us two more pieces of *good news...*

1 **Repetition decreases resistance.**
The same as making a path through a field of wheat, the first time you leave a slight trace...
Repeat your route many times and you've made a pathway that is larger and easier to negotiate. So with your brain cells, you've made a new habit which becomes easier to repeat.

Therefore:
REPETITION INCREASES
the likelihood of REPETITION.

2 Professor Anokhin of Moscow University researched **the information processing capabilities of the brain and found them to be „limitless".** He calculated the number of possible patterns your 1,000,000,000,000 brain cells could make as:
One followed by 10 ½ million kilometres of typewritten 'o's

Just about INFINITE!
IMPRESSED?!

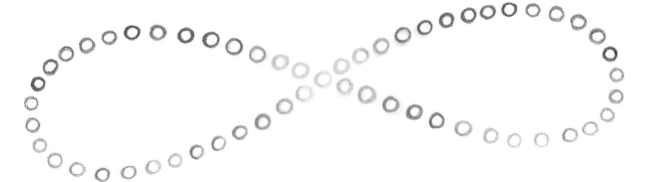

Practice makes . . . . .permenant!

So, to *learn* how to learn and think well ...

You need to:

1
USE THE SKILLS OF YOUR WHOLE BRAIN (See page 21).

2
USE YOUR BRAIN'S NATURAL ASSOCIATIVE „bloom" and „flow" to retain and recall information. (pages 26 & 27)

3
REPEAT (in an variety of ways using ALL your senses) to create new patterns (page 31) and

4
USE a MIND MAP as a way of accomplishing 1-3. (Coming up next)

What a way to GET AHEAD!

HIGHLIGHTS:

- 12 steps to make a Mind Map

- Compare linear & radiant thinking

- 12 questions with answers

MINDMAPS®

To introduce you to Mind Maps:

First there will be an EXAMPLE and we'll tell you how to „read" it.

Then we will show you HOW to make a Mind Map in 12 easy steps, and explain WHY each „LAW" is important for your MENTAL FREEDOM.

Next we will let you COMPARE a Mind Map with the TRADITIONAL method of note making to see which uses MORE of your WHOLE BRAIN.

Then we answer 12 QUESTIONS, you may have about Mind Maps and

finally we will both REVIEW the Mind Map Laws

MIND MAPS®

- use your whole-brain skills
- use the „flow" and „bloom" of association
- reflect the way your brain works, looks and is constructed
- are the language of your brain

Said in Mind Map form

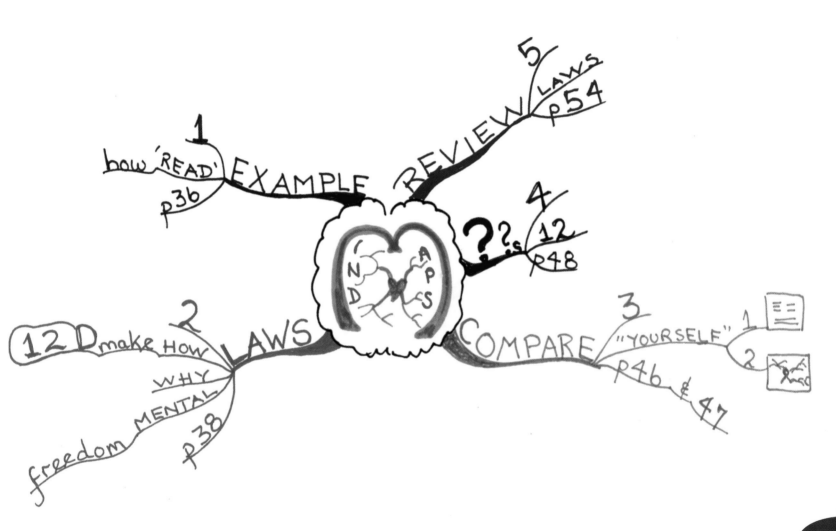

Learn how to read Mind Maps®

First, an example of a special voyage Mind Map.

How to read
this Mind Map:

1

Start in the centre
That is the focus of the Mind Map.
In this case the Ocean Liner Queen
Elizabeth 2 (QE2) on the high seas!

2

Next, **read the „key words"** which
CONNECT to the central image.
They are the equivalent of Chapter
Headings, and give you the **MAIN
THEMES or TOPICS** of the Mind Map.

In this Mind Map they are: the FOOD—
making EXERCISE even more necessary;
the PEOPLE; the extra SPECIAL activities
and the incredible indelible MEMORIES
of the VOYAGE.

3

**Read out from the centre on each
branch.**
This provides greater levels of
associated detail and „triggers" to aid
the memory of the whole voyage.

4

Notice any **links** between the
branches.

Wasn't that
easy?

You are getting ahead! Now **HOW** to
Mind Map...One of the really great things
about Mind Mapping, is that for every law
there is a very good BrainFriendly reason.
Mind Maps MAKE SENSE. OK?
Then we'll tell you **HOW to MIND MAP!**

How to make
Mind Maps®
and why these „laws"
are so important

In 12 simple steps you will know the „how" & the „why".

How:

Why:

Take a **BLANK** piece of paper this size or larger. Preferably use a Mind Map Pad.

Blank paper allows 360° of **freedom to express** the full range of your cortical skills, whereas pre-drawn lines restrict the natural flow of your thoughts.

Use the paper **LANDSCAPE** (on its side).

Words and images have more **LATERAL space**, so they don't bump into the margins as quickly.

How:

Why:

START in the **CENTRE**

Thoughts START in the CENTRE of our **mental world.** The Mind Map page **reflects** this.

Make a **CENTRAL IMAGE** that personally represents the topic about which you are writing/thinking. Also:
- Use **at least 3 colours** in the image

- Keep the height and width of the **central image to approx 2" or 5 cm.**

- Leave the image **OPEN** (do not use a frame)

„**A picture is worth a thousand words".** It opens up associations, focuses the thought, is fun and results in better recall.
- **Colours stimulate** the right cortical activitiy of imagination as well as capturing and holding attention.
- This size gives **plenty of space** for the rest of your Mind Map. The image has its own unique shape.
- A frame makes the centre a monotony of shape. A **free image** is more memorable and enjoyable.

EXAMPLE:
The topic of this Mind Map is „**HAPPINESS"** (This image of two people running along a beach represents „Happiness" to us.) Now, we'll start to build it up.

How:

The **MAIN THEMES** around the **Central Image** are like the chapter headings of a book. Imagine you are going to write a book on „Happiness". One of the themes coud be **„FAMILY".**

● THIS WORD is **PRINTED.**

● **PLACED on a LINE** of the **SAME LENGTH.**

● The **CENTRAL LINES** are thick, curved and **ORGANIC** ie (like your arm joining your body, or the branch of a tree to the trunk).

● **CONNECTED** directly **to the CENTRAL IMAGE.**

Why:

The **main themes,** connected to the Central Image on the main branches, allow their relative importance to be seen.

● **PRINTING** (versus joined up writing) allows the brain to photograph the image and thus gives easier reading and more immediate recall.

● **Word length = Line length,** as extra line **dis**connects thoughts, whereas the same length accentuates the connection.

● **Curved lines** give visual rhythm and variety and so are **easier to remember,** more pleasant to do and **less boring!** Thicker central lines show importance.

● **Connected** to the image because the brain works **by association**. Not by separated disconnected lists.

How:

Add other **MAIN THEME BRANCHES,** by imaging other „chapter headings"

Why:

So all your **MAIN THEMES** stand out clearly, and can trigger your subsequent connecting thoughts.

We've added 2 more and left 2 for you.REMEMBER to **PRINT** the word and make it fit the line.

How:

Why:

Start to add a **SECOND level of thought.**
These words or images are linked to the main branch that triggered them.

REMEMBER:

● Lines connect and are now thinner

● Words PRINTED but may be lower case, (like these letters).

Your initial words and images **stimulate associations.** Attach those words to whatever word or image triggerd them. Allow the 'random' movement of your thought, you do not have to „finish" one branch before moving on.
● Connected lines create **relationships** and a **structure.** They also demonstrate the level of **importance**, as from a branch to a twig.
● The **size and style** of the letters provides additional data about their **importance** and meaning.

Add a **THIRD or FOURTH level** of data, as thoughts come to you. Use **IMAGES** as much as you can, instead of, or in addition to words.Allow your thoughts to come FREELY, meaning you „hop about" the Mind Map as the links and associations occur to you.

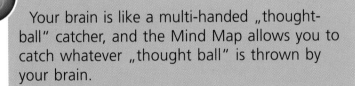

Your brain is like a multi-handed „thought-ball" catcher, and the Mind Map allows you to catch whatever „thought ball" is thrown by your brain.

Add DIMENSION to your Mind Maps. Box and add depth around the word or image.

To make **IMPORTANT POINTS** stand out.

Add some more of your own branches, words and images to this Mind Map.

How:

Sometimes enclose **branches** of a Mind Map **with outlines in colours**, HUG the shape of the branch

- USE different colours and styles

- Add ARROWS and CODES between information to show the connection.

Make each Mind Map a little more:
- beautiful,
  - artistic,
    - colourful,
      - imaginative and
        - dimensional.

Have FUN!
Add a little humour, exagGeration or absurdity wherever you can.

Why:

The **OUTLINES** will create **UNIQUE** shapes, (as you find in the clouds,) and will aid your memory.

- They can also show connection between branches, by using the same colour or style of outline.
- These provide immediate visual linking. They can also encourage follow-up and remind you of action you need to take.

Your eye/brain will be attracted to your Mind Map.
- It will be easier to remember.
- It will be more attractive to you (and to others as well.)

Your brain will delight in getting the MAXIMUM enjoyment from this process, and will learn faster and recall more effectively. Studying becomes much more enjoyable.

Got it?!

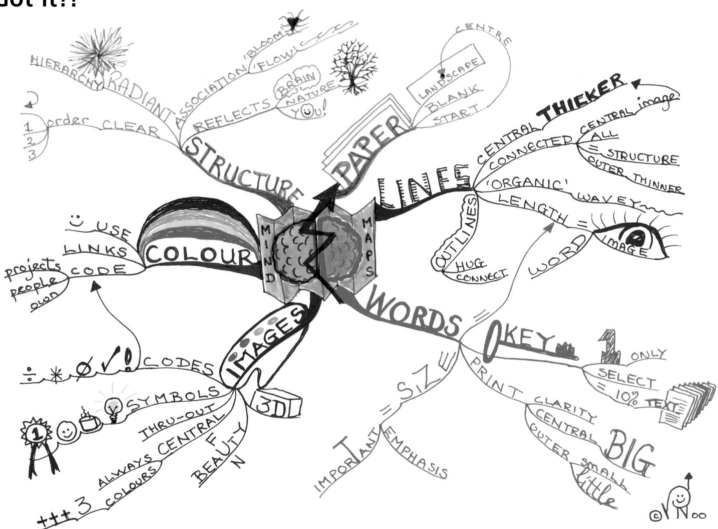

On the next page do your own first Mind Map (as a comparison with UGO „Yourself 1". Don't look back yet!)

Using **„YOURSELF"** as the topic, make a quick central image that represents you. Continue, as you did with the LOVE & WATER UGOs, and flow the branches out. This is a HIGH SPEED UGO (for 5 mins) your mind gives you words and images to Mind Map. READY? GO?

*YOUR*self
description 2

NOW you can turn back to page 15 – „YOURSELF 1"

COMPARE the DIFFERENCES with „YOURSELF 2" in :
- Using the skills of your whole brain (left and right),

- Using associative functions of your brain („bloom" & „flow")
- The quantity of information you generated.

Place a ✔ in the column under „Yourself" linear or Mind Map.

Did you use?	„YOURSELF" linear	„YOURSELF" Mind Map
LISTS		
LOGIC		
LINES		
WORDS		
NUMBERS		
ORDER		
RHYTHM		
SPACE		
DAY DREAMING		
IMAGINATION (IMAGES)		
COLOUR		
OVERVIEW		
ASSOCIATION		

Was it?	„YOURSELF" linear	„YOURSELF" Mind Map
FUN		
FLOWING		
EASY		
ATTRACTIVE		
MEMORABLE		
CONCENTRATED		
FOCUSED		
EFFICIENT		
DETAILED		

Are there more ✔'s in the Mind Map Column?

12 Questions
often asked...
(and the answers)

To help you with your next Mind Maps,
We will answer some ?'s people often ask.

What makes a
good Key word?

? Out of 100 written words in standard notes only 10 are REALLY IMPORTANT. These are called the KEY WORDS: The key words are usually **nouns** or **very strong action words** eg: cage, cricket, feed, love, sing, legs, dead. (from Kusa Hibari - Use Your Head) They are the words that **bring back** to you the precise images and events that you want to remember.

Why only
1 word
per line?

? Because each word and image has millions of possible associations. Therefore, if you give it its own freedom you will get more ideas from it, and be able to remember it more clearly.

What *supplies* do I need?

?
Large and small **Mind Mapping® Pads** (Good Qualitiy **blank white paper** that takes the colour well) and

● Thin and thicker **PENS** as well as **Highlighters** in different colours.

Your brain will think your're playing, while you are learning all the time.

How can I use *colours?*

?
You can **use them to**:
● clearly identify the **branches,**
● code **themes** that have several branches,
● code a **topic** as it appears on different branches,
● code **individuals** attending a meeting,
● code different **dates** or **levels** of information,
● code different **projects**
● collect ideas and show **connections**
● make it **even** more **beautiful.**

When I get „*stuck"*, what should I do?

?
Your **brain NATURALLY loves to complete things,** so add some blank lines – it will WANT to fill them in. Also, remind yourself that EVERY word could be the centre of a Mind Map (like the LOVE UGO).You have **infinite possibilities for associating.**

How do I select my *Main Branch* words?

? Remember to think of the Mind Map as a general outline for a book on that topic. Your Main Branch word/images will always be equivalent to **chapter headings.** They are the word/images that encompass a number of other ideas within them.

For example in the Mind Map on Happiness we used: FAMILY; FOOD; NATURE; and you added, _____; _____ as the Basic Ordering Ideas.

What if the *same word* is repeated many times in my Mind Map®?

? This is good because you will have discovered a major theme or **new direction** in your Mind Map. Each occurrrence of the word/image represents another hook or connection and may create a new frame of reference.

What do I do if I have „*stupid*" thoughts?

? Allow **ALL thoughts,** words, images or feelings that come to be attached to the word or image which „triggered" them. So called „stupid" thoughts produce some of the most insightful, original and creative ideas. The more you add to your Mind Map (most particularly in the initial burst, creative stage) the more sense things that initially seemed to be „stupid" will make. The stupid ideas are often your **guides to innovative thinking.** Wait for a later stage in your Mind Map before considering what editing, refinement or changes you may want to make.

Can a Mind Map improve my *creativity?*

? YES! Just place the topic, problem or need as your central image, and **„Bloom"** out all associated thoughts and ideas. Then **„Flow"** some of the „Bloomed" words two or three levels further out. Take a break and see what you have created!

Will you help me
with symbols?

Copy the symbols in the spaces.

? Symbols are often very personal, so start creating and playing with your own symbols for common objects, people, projects and concepts. Here are some ideas for you to copy or adapt.

How do I take
Mind Map notes?

Follow this Mind Map, and see an additional explanation on pages 71 & 74.

pages 71 & 74.

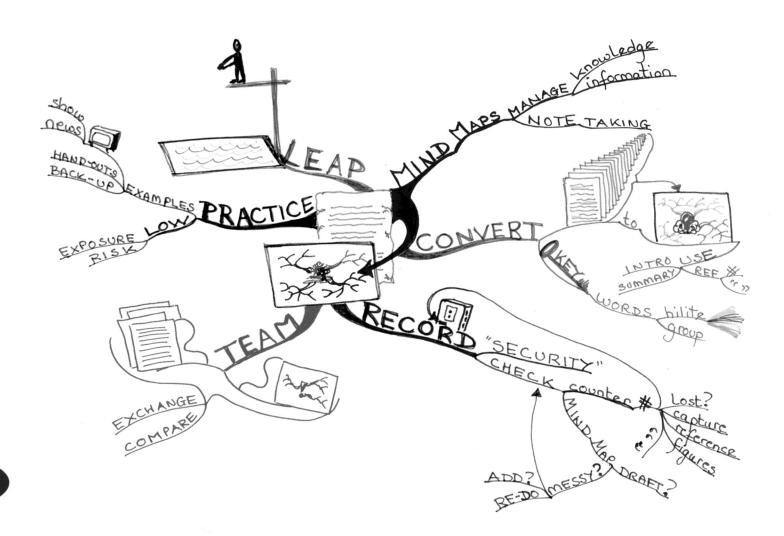

When does a
Mind Map end?

?

In one sense.. **NEVER!!**
(or when You choose to stop!)
Because every word or image could be
the centre of another Mind Map,
demonstrating that your associatve
ability is, by definition, limitless.

What a contrast to what one can normally generate in linear form!

The Mind Map gives a far more accurate
reflection of your INTELLIGENCE:
IMAGINE!
A Mind Map is an INFINTE REFLECTION OF
YOUR LIMITLESS INTELLIGENCE.

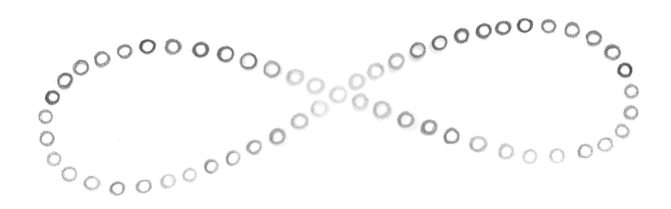

Use **BLANK** paper.

Turn the paper **SIDEWAYS**.

Start in the **CENTRE**.

Make a **COLOURFUL IMAGE** to represent the **topic** of the Mind Map.

Add the **MAIN THEMES** (like chapter headings) and place them:
- **One** word or image
- **PRINTED**
- **ON an organic (wavey) line**
- line is **CONNECTED**
- line is **THICKER** towards the centre.

BRANCH off the main themes.

SECOND levels of thought are added.

Let us review the
Mind Mapping
Laws

Continue with **THIRD** and **FOURTH levels** as the thoughts flow.

Incorporate:
- KEY WORDS
- SYMBOLS and
- DIMENSION
- with ARROWS
- and CODES!*)

OUTLINE or enclose the branches.

Make each Mind Map more filled with **BEAUTY.**

... and HAVE FUN!

54

**Now you recap the Mind Map
Laws in Mind Map form here:**

So we could say that in your magnificent BIO-COMPUTER the **BRAIN CELL** is like the **HARDWARE**; the **BRAIN SKILLS Left & Right** and **ASSOCIATIVE** functions are like the **Disc Operating System**; and **Mind Maps** are the **SOFTWARE** for the hardware of your BIO-COMPUTER.

BRILLIANT!

HIGHLIGHTS:

- 14 day
  „Just Do It!" programme

- 12 steps to the
  radiant thinking habit

- 36 brain problems solved

The JUST DO IT!
Programme

The next pages provide a PROGRAMME with examples of, and practice for Mind Mapping in different situations. This will help to make the process more NATURAL for you, as you begin to Just Do It!

Research shows you need at least 14 – 21 days to create a new habit, so follow this programme and watch your new habit **AND** your potential grow!

- NOTE MAKING
  Some Mind Maps help you to take information OUT of your head...

- NOTE TAKING
  Some Mind Maps help you to put information IN to your head...

- ALL Mind Maps help you to GET AHEAD!

From linear to radiant
Mind Mapping in a
2 week programme

DAY 1   EXPAND a MIND MAP

DAY 2   UN-SCRAMBLE a shopping list into a MIND MAP

DAY 3   WRITE a Letter from a MIND MAP

DAY 4   CONVERT a list for a trip or party to a MIND MAP

DAY 5   MAKE NOTES for a speech, essay or important conversation with a MIND MAP

DAY 6   PLAY and RELAX. Plan your weekend with a MIND MAP

DAY 7   EXPLORE a topic of interest or a hobby with a MIND MAP

DAY 8   TAKE notes from a BOOK or report on a MIND MAP

DAY 9   TAKE notes from a TV show or meeting with a MIND MAP

DAY 10   DECIDE an issue with a MIND MAP

DAY 11   BRAINBLOOM a topic with a MIND MAP

DAY 12   PLAN the items, order and timing of a project with a MIND MAP

Day 13   MIND MAP your rewards and special treats

DAY 14   MIND MAP all the ways you like to play, have fun & CELEBRATE

...or said in a
Mind Map

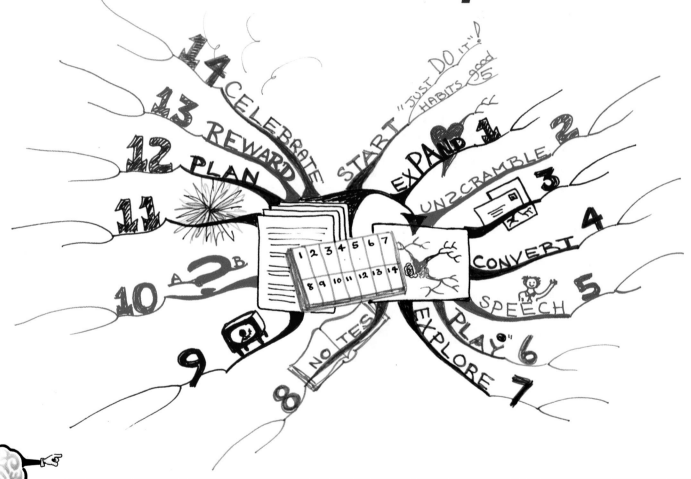

By the day number, write the date and ✔ when done.

Make the Mind Map habit
easy as you
Just Do It.

6 Steps to a Radiant Habit:

1 Buy an enticing array of good **coloured pens** in fine, medium and highlighter thickness.

2 Have LARGE and regular sized, good **quality BLANK paper** in Mind Map Pads on your desk or table.

3 Convert some important existing **lists** (ie shopping, birthday, holiday, things to do etc.) **to Mind Maps.** Use them regularly as „Check Maps".

4 Catch those **'random' and rapid thoughts** on 'first draft' Mind Maps. Aggregate the thoughts by highlighter colours. When necessary re-do the Mind Map.

5 Put Mind Maps in your office, study, kitchen, to remind you to make them, but …

6 OOPS, if you only remember to MIND MAP **after** you've begun your (linear) notes, START right then to MIND MAP. Afterward go back and highlight the KEY words from your previous notes. Add these word to the appropiate branches on your MIND MAP. Soon Mind Mapping will become a natural habit.

Just Do It …
Get Ahead!

DAY 1 *Expanding*

Make more of a Mind Map from the UGO you did on page 26. Copy your 10 words on the 10 branches here. Select 3 words, then connect thoughts by word and/or image, do a „flow" of associations. Follow our example:

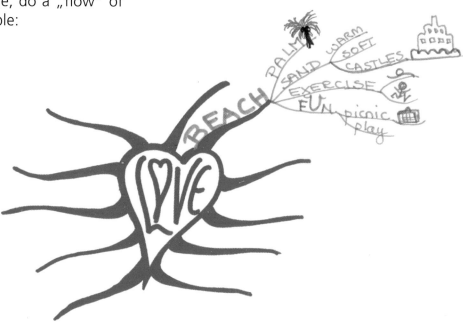

Now it has expanded into a Mind Map!

Remember, a Mind Map is like a multi-handed „Thought-ball" catcher. It gives you a place to keep all your Great Thoughts and Ideas as they pop into your head.

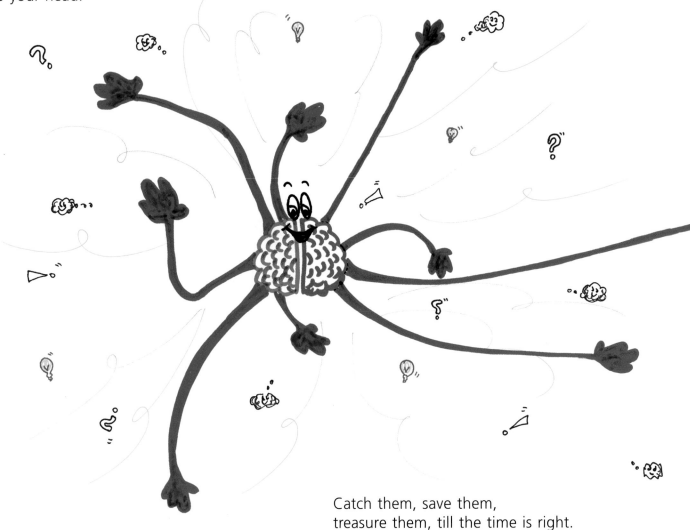

Catch them, save them,
treasure them, till the time is right.

DAY 2 *Unscrambling*

Unscramble the shopping list below on to the
Mind Map, (We've started you off…)

Fish Food
Bacon
Cheese
Bread
Butter
Apples
Tomatoes
Newspaper
Soap
Batteries
Cake
Magazine
Dog food
Note paper
Wine
Lettuce
Milk
Toilet paper
Chicken
Eggs

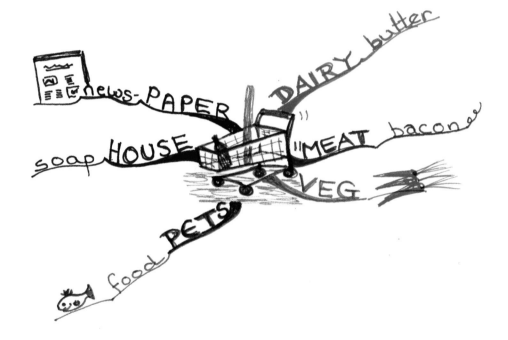

The list is • mixed up • easy to forget
• easy to overlook something.

Whereas the Mind Map is • easy to read • easy to
add to • time saving • more efficient • and fun!

Note making

To prepare for Day 3's activity, we'll look at:
Taking information from your head OUT
(Note Making).

Have you ever:

● Sent a letter to a friend or acquaintance and
FORGOTTEN to include one of the main
reasons for writing the letter?

● Gone in to make several important points to
your supervisor (teacher or friend) and left
out one of the most important ones?

● Had a „Great Idea" while you were planning
a speech or report, but couldn't remember it
when you needed it?

YES!?!
hurumph

Then...

Make a Mini-Mind Map to capture your Quick Thoughts

Make a Mini-Mind Map whenever
you want to:

● capture a few thoughts or ideas
● plan a small project
● order your „TO DO" things for the day
● remember items to say to a friend
● organise your thougts
● empty your head of „chatter".

In most instances where you would normally
use a list, a Mini-Mind Map will serve you
better.

Your multi-handed Thought-Ball catcher will
catch all those thoughts that just „float"
through and out of your head. Taking care of
all these problems and needs.

DAY 3 *Writing*

Prepare to write a letter to a friend or colleague. What are the main points to communicte?

Remember the Mind Map Laws…
Gather your ideas first, **then** put them in order.

DAY 4 *Converting*

Plan a Trip or a Party.

List things to do here: Convert the list to a Mind Map here:

One thought „triggers" another. You see the
connections & relationships. Did the Mind Map
help you to think of extra items?

How to prepare a
speech using
a Mind Map

A Mind Map makes effective speaking much easier and more enjoyable. It lets you 'be yourself'.

Put your topic in the **centre**.

Let all your „thought-balls" fly, and catch them on your Mind Map branches as (and where) they come.

When you feel „done", **sequence** the branches – your beginning, middle and end – by numbering them.

RE-do the Mind Map if you feel it would help.

Add how long you want to spend on any branch, by adding the minutes. Note any handouts or audiovideo use on the branch with a symbol.

DAY 5 *Speaking*

Prepare to make a „speech" for any reason, where you need to 'present' to one person up to 100 people, eg:

● comment on a product,
● tell a story
● present your side of an argument,
● convince someone of your point of view,
● influence a special friend in your life

MIND MAP your Speech here:

DAY 6 *Playing & relaxing*

Organise your weekend with a Mind Map.

DAY 7 *Exploring*

Explore a topic of interest or a
hobby with a Mind Map.

Congratulations!
You ar half way through the
„Just Do It" Mind Map programme.

Putting information
into your head
Note taking

Here we'll deal with two situations:
- from the **printed word,** eg. written notes, books, reports, computers, etc.,
- from the **spoken word,** eg. lectures, speeches, TV shows, mentors, meetings, conversations, panels, discussions etc.

First, Note TAKING from the PRINTED word (eg. Books, Magazines, Reprts)

1 The idea for your **CENTRAL IMAGE** may be stimulated by the covers, logos or any other graphics or images from the material you are reading.

2 The **MAJOR BRANCHES** could be supplied by:
- Chapter Headings or Division Headings
- Goals, Teachers or yours
- Questions or the
- Index

3 **Browse and RANGE READ*** the information adding layers of detail as needed.

4 Remember to **SELECT** the information you need and REJECT that which you don't.

5 **HIGHLIGHT** the KEY WORDS which will provide the „triggers" to large quantities of additional data.

*See Tony Buzans's „Speed & Range Reading".

*A whale of a communicator
by Mowgli from Synapsia '2
(the Brain Club Journal)

The New Scientist of 10 March 1990 reports that a Canadian scientist has found that killer whales speak a number of different languages in a number of different dialects. The difference between the dialects can be as small as those distinguishing regional dialects of national language, or can be as large as those between European and Asian languages.

SUPER-INTELLIGENT LINGUISTIC CLUB

This finding places the whales in the super-intelligent linguistic club among mammals – club that includes humans, major primates and harbour seals. (Current research suggest that sound produced by the other mammals are determined genetically although there is a growing band of researchers who consider that animals are far more linguistically intelligent than we have previously assumed, and are specieswide and individually creative in their communication).

John Fort, curator of Marine Mammals at the Vancouver Public Aquarium in British Columbia, has been studying communication between killer whales for a decade. He observes that killer whale dialects are made of the whistles and calls the animals use when communicating underwater. These calls are quite distinct from the high energy, sonar-like 'click' that the whales emit when navigating by echo-location.

Killer whales are actually members of the Dolphin family, and are the largest in that family Their name is a misnomer, there being no report that one has ever attacked a human – on the contrary there are an increasing number of records that these whales, like dolphins, have often helped humans.

WHISTLING WHALES

Perhaps we in The Brain Club could start a movement to have them renamed – perhaps the Whistler Whale/ whistling whales would be more appropriate, apart from being more onomatopoeic. Synapsia will henceforth refer to them by this name.

Whistling whales are found in all the major oceans of the word, from the warmest in the tropics to the coldest in the North and South Poles. The largest concentrations are found off the coastal regions of the cool countries, including Iceland and Canada.

The population Ford studied numbered approx. 350 who live for the entire year off the coats of British Columbia and northern Washington State in America. The whales have formed two separate communities which roam through adjacent territories.

The 'northern community', which consists of 16 family groups, or 'pods', ranges from mid-Vancouver Island north to the south east top of Alaska. The members of the smaller 'southern community' divided themselves into three pods and wander from the border of the northern community all the way south into Puget Sound and Grays Harbour.

Fortunately, most sounds produced by whistling whales are within the range of human hearing. Ford's research is therefore easy to carry out-he simply dangles a hydrophone over the side of the boat, and amplifies the sounds electronically, recording them on a tape.

Through his research Ford has been able to identify the dialect of each pod. He has found that, on average, a pod makes twelve discreet calls. Each member of the pod is able to, and does, produce the full set of whistles and calls. The system of these whistles and calls is different, both quantitatively and qualitatively, from those of other dolphins and whales.

Most calls are used only within a pod, but sometimes one or more are common between pods.

COMMON ANCESTORS

Interestingly, Ford has found that these dialects are passed from generation-to-generation within each pod, leading him to speculate that groups which share calls probably descended from a common ancestor or ancestors. The more calls two pods have in common the closer the family relationship.

This phylo-genetic link between dialect and pod has enabled ford to estimate how long it takes for a separate dialect to emerge. „The rate of change appears to be very slow", he says. „It (a dialect) must require centuries to develop" the implication is that some dialects could be thousands of years old,

One new focus of Ford's research has been the correlation between the behaviour of whistling whales and the calls they make. So far he has not found that calls are faster, high in pitch, and more frequent when an animal is excited.

Ford currently believes that taken together the calls form an „elaborate code of pod identity" which enables Whistler Whales to identify the fellow members of their pod. This is especially important for keeping the 'family' together when collections of pods, known as 'super pods' swim together.

So far, Ford has not been able to identify a grammatical structure in Whistler Whale communication. But he impressed by it's acoustic sophistication:" They seem to have a highly developed, efficient way of communicating that is something we can only partly understand at this point" he says. „I think as time goes on, we will get a much better appreciation of just how remarkably adapted whales are to their unique environment."

DAY 8 *Note taking*

You'll have less pages of notes making it easier to learn and you'll 'save a tree'!

- Read the text p72.
- HIGHLIGHT the KEY WORDS.
- Make a Mind Map here.

Note taking
from the spoken word

To prepare you for Day 9 let's talk about: Note TAKING from the SPOKEN word (eg. Speech, TV show, meeting, story)

 Get your **CENTRAL IMAGE** from the title, theme or topic of the speech or show.

It helps to have your **MAIN BRANCHES already prepared.** This may be discovered by ASKING the speaker for the main TOPICS, or thinking what you want to get out of it.

 To build up your SKILL and CONFIDENCE you may want to try the following:

● Start with a „**low-risk" activity,** which has backup material provided, a T.V. show or the news is a good idea.

● Create a Mind Map from your **linear notes, highlighting the KEY words** for your main branches. Attach your 1 page Mind Map to your linear notes and use your Mind Map as a cover review.

● **Work with a „buddy".** One make a Mind Map, one make linear notes. Compare after the lecture.

● As a back up use a small **tape recorder.** If you feel you are getting „behind", „lost" or „in a mess" note the tape counter number of that moment. Also note the tape counter number of any good „quote" formula or important information that you may have missed. Then check back on the tape and add any of these to your Mind Map after the presentation.

4 If you wish to RE-DO or RE-ORDER your Mind Map because it looks „**MESSY"**, consider what MESSY means. Is it from the LOOK or the ORGANISATION of the information? (Linear notes may LOOK NEAT, but INFORMATIONALLY they may be messy, because it is hard to get the information back from them at a glance. A hurried Mind Map may look messy, but informationally it is still NEATER and CLEARER.) You can always make your Mind Map more beautiful and well organised when your review or re-do it. Keep your Mind Maps in topic folders. If you have redone your Mind Map then you keep the old one too, as it holds the memories of the occasion.

5 Sometimes you are not sure what the speech is about. In this case, make the branches around an empty space for the Central Image. When (if) it becomes clear, draw in the Central Image.

6 The most important themes and KEY words can be moved from many specific, detailed Mind Maps on to a **MASTER MIND MAP.** This can be a magnificent REVIEW process and also can show the CONNECTIONS and RELATIONS between information, even from different disciplines.

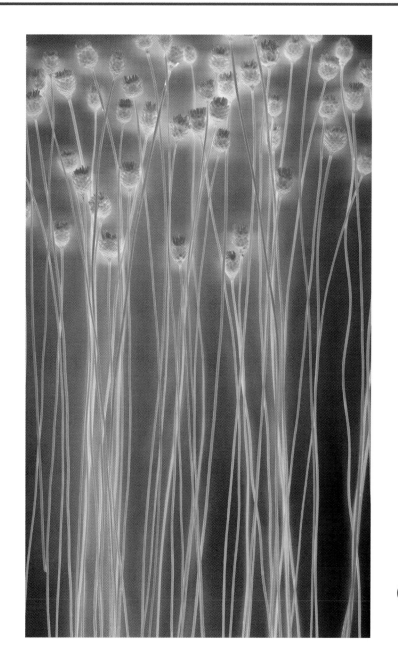

DAY 9 *Note taking*

Note Taking becomes fast, fun and easily memorable with Mind Maps.

Make a Mind Map from the spoken word. Select:
● a meeting
● a TV show or Documentary
● a story on the radio
● a speech or presentation
● a class or lecture.

Thinking *skills*
with Mind Maps®

For Days 10, 11 and 12 we will be using the „IN"
and „OUT" together:

To create the BrainFriendly thinking skills to assist:

● DECISION MAKING

● BRAINBLOOMING

● PLANNING and PRIORITISING

77

Making *decisions*
with Mind Maps®

A Mind Map can help you make decisions, for example it can help clarify the go/no go; yes/no; a/b choices about an issue [In this example we looked at the positives and negatives (good/bad) of taking (yes) or not taking (no) a job.]

The more information you place on a Mind Map the more the necessary decision will become apparent. If it is still in the balance then either choice may be O.K.

DAY 10 *Deciding*

Select an issue about which you
need to decide, and do your Mind
Map on this page:

BEWARE –
there is a third choice ... that of „C" – to do
NEITHER „A" or „B"!
WATCH OUT for (and don't make) this CHOICE.

A Mind Map
can also help with
generating new ideas.

Traditionally this has been called a **„brain-storm"**, a process of generating all possible ideas, associations and links you have about a topic, then taking them from your brain and 'raining' them on to the paper.

In Get Ahead we call a brain-storm a **„BrainBloom"**. It allows the great blossoming, flowering, associating, connecting and developing of your thoughts, ideas, and facts, to be captured in their radiant beauty.

To get started you may want to ask:

WHERE WHO WHY WHAT HOW WHEN

80

DAY 11
BrainBlooming

Pick an issue that:
- you want to explore
- you know a lot about
- is of topical interest

and do a „BrainBloom" around it...

Next page shows an example.

Here is an **example** of a **brain bloom** on the topic „education"

DAY 12 *Planning*

Plan some event that is soon to occur. Let your thoughts flow. When you have finished your Mind Map order and proritise the items.

It is so helpful to have the entire plan on one sheet of paper, and so satisfying to ✔ items off when completed.

See example on next page.

Planning
with Mind Maps®

A Mind Map makes:

- ORGANISING
- PLANNING
- PRIORITISING and
- TIME MANAGMENT

much easier!

The order of events can be coded by dates with the initials of the person responsible, or just prioritised.

Let's have a 50th birthday party as an example:

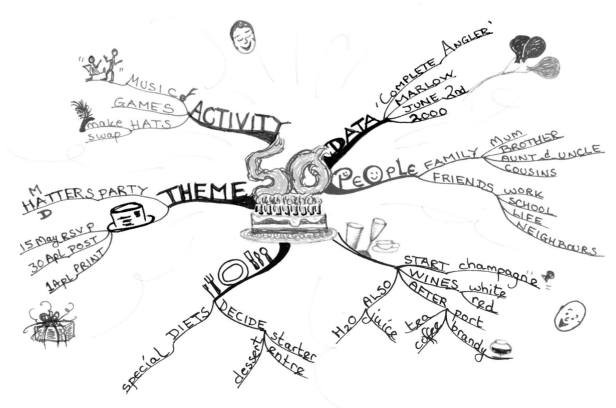

DAY 13 *Rewarding*

Mind Map all the things you like
to do or have as special treats or
rewards.

DAY 14
Celebrating

You have Just Do(ne) It!
Mind Map all the ways you like to
play, have fun and CELEBRATE!

You've
got it!

6 steps to
Radiant Thinking...

To keep stepping in the right direction:

1 Have your Mind Mapping paper and pens colorfully, invitingly **accessible.**

2 Start with the Mind Maps that you find **easiest**, most **useful** and most **fun** to do.

3 Show off and **explain** your Mind Maps to friends, family members and colleagues when ever possible.

4 **Teach** your partner, family or group to Mind Map so you may plan, discuss and communicate with them.

5 In an **emergency** (a rush or only one colour available) Mind Map **anyway** and add colour underlines, boxes or highlighter codes later.

6 Increase the use of **beauty, images, codes, and symbols** by mimicking good examples.

Half your brain to your WHOLE brain!

You have now stepped over from the **linear** (traditional method) to **radiant Mind Maps.**

Watch out!
Mind Maps®
are about and they
attract attention...

A very shy gentleman met the lady of his dreams because she asked him about his Mind Map®, and he became so involved explaining it, he **forgot** his **shyness**!

Yet another received a very **good promotion** because the Mind Maps® made visible his creativity!

Another person received much **appreciation** when her Mind Map® notes of a very complex meeting were noticed and she was able to describe succinctly the major points.

A Mind Mapping® student had other students stopping her in the school corridors asking to learn to Mind Map® so they could, like her, get **better grades and marks**!.

At a conference a Mind Mapper® was able to give **clear reviews** of each of the presentations, much to the appreciation of the rest of the delegates.

Mind Maps® have been the way that several people have asked their partners to marry them... and they have all said „Yes!"

Now that you have stepped over, lets look back

With your Mind Mapping software programme installed in your brain, and your owner's & user's manual now provided. Look back to the benchmarks from the start of your journey.

- Remember the problems with your brain
- Remember and goals for your brain (p13) Go back and:
- ✔ the problems now being dealt with.
- ✔ the goals you are now achieving.

Return to page 16 „Have you ever been taught how to…? See the pages listed if you would like to review where we addressed all these issues.

- **Organise thoughts :** pages 25; 38-44; 48; 50; 63-64; 67; 77-78; 83; 91
- **Let thoughts flow:** pages 26-27; 38-44; 49; 50; 53; 61-62; 91
- **Prepare a speech:** pages 26; 46; 67; 91
- **Gather information:** pages 71; 74-75; 81; 91
- **Improve your memory:** pages 28; 31; 38-44; 51; 91
- **Make studying fun:** pages 24; 32; 38-44; 51; 71; 91
- **Make a decision:** pages 77-79; 91

> You have learned:
> how you learn
> making all learning
> and thinking
> easier.

You can them ✔ ALL off!

If you also shared some of the problems listed on p14, here are brief explanations of how a Mind Map® can help you handle them. For simplicity, we have grouped them as per this Mind Map:

EXAMS
STUDY
CONCENTRATE
MOTIVATE
REMEMBER
facts RECALL
!PROCRASTINATE
LEARN

START
ORGANISE
LOGICAL
CREATIVE
BRAIN-STORM   BLOOM
STOP!
THINK

PROBLEMS
GOALS

EFFECTIVE
PUBLIC
FREEDOM
YOURSELF
COMMUNICATE

ANALYSE   **PROBLEM**
SOLVE
DECIDE

PLAN
PRIORITISE
PREPARE
DELEGATE
FOLLOW-UP

KNOWLEDGE   TIME
INFORMATION   PROJECTS
"TODO"
MANAGE

36 Problems Solved!

36 problems solved

THINKING –

start; organise; logical; creative; brain-storm;
BrainBloom; stop!
From getting started to stopping, you'll find the Mind Map process can assist the flow; quantity; quality; clarity, creativity and organisation of your thoughts. It makes thinking a delight!

COMMUNICATING –

effective & / or public speaking;
freedom; be yourself.
Having the key points you wish to make in a flexible structure on your Mind Map, allows you to be sure you cover every thing, while addressing the needs of the person or group. It is easy to remember and to keep your place. Best of all, it gives you the freedom to be yourself!

PLANNING –

prioritise; prepare; delegate; follow-up.
All the things to be done can be seen on one page, making any gaps or overlaps apparent. The same Mind Map facilitates the prioritising; preparing; delegating and time management of all aspects. Completion and follow-up are monitored, ensuring an effective plan is achieved.

MANAGING –

knowledge; information; time; projects; "to-dos"
Large quantities of information can be available as accessible knowledge through software linked Mind Maps. From daily "to-dos" to a large project you can be aware of the overview, therefore allocating time appropriately.

PROBLEM SOLVING –

analyse; decide.
Seeing all aspects, facts, feelings, and repercussions of a problem on a one page Mind Map is a great aid to you in analyzing and therefore assessing and choosing the best solution. It enables you to see the whole picture at a glance.

LEARNING –

study; exams; concentrate; motivate;
remember and recall facts; procrastinate.
Many pages of linear notes can be condensed into a Mega-Mind Map. This makes review for, and recall during exams much easier. The flow, fun, speed, colour and images entice and maintain the focus of your attention. This aides concentration, overcomes procrastination, and enhances motivation.

"What is that"?

If someone asks you about your Mind Maps®, this is what you could tell them! Simply say that it is a note taking/making system:

- Similar to that used by: Einstein; Churchill; Leonardo da Vinici; Buckminister Fuller; Mark Twain; Walt Disney and most of the people considered to have „**Great Brains"**.

- Based on the latest **information** on **How** and **Why** your **brain functions**, and the **skills** that are compatible with it.

- That matches the language of your mind.

- That facilitates the learning & thinking process.

- That **millions of people** from 5 years old to Company Directors, parents and government leaders are using it... including your good self.

And,
by the way,
what kind of
a **system** do
they use?!?!!

Can you take one more piece of Amazing and Good News?

In the 1950s it was assumed the use of our brain's ability was about ... **50%**

In the 1960s it was reduced to ... **25%**

In the 1970s a further dramatic reduction to ... **10%**

And in the 1980s another drop to ... **4%**

And in the 1990s ... down to ... **1%**

and now, less then ... **1%**

Did we say this was supposed to be good News?!

YES, YES, YES!

This news shows that we are increasingly discovering that everyone's basic ability is **far greater** than we had previously thought. **(And that includes yours!)**

Consider what „**Great Whole-Brain"** users have achieved in these areas.

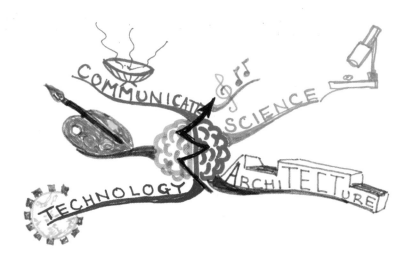

So, If we add only **1%**
we will have more than **DOUBLED**
our active use of our amazing
brain's ability and with
Mind Maps® it is easy to...

Get Ahead
with
Mind Maps®!

**Cerebrate!*

You have
Got Ahead!

*The Joyous celebration of your magnificent cerebal capabilities.

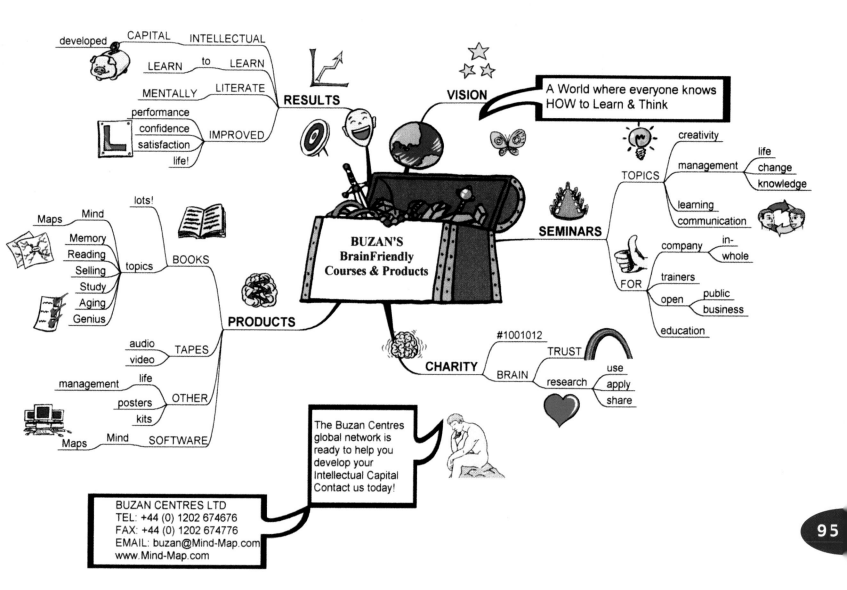

developed — CAPITAL — INTELLECTUAL

LEARN — to — LEARN

MENTALLY — LITERATE

RESULTS

performance
confidence — IMPROVED
satisfaction
life!

VISION

A World where everyone knows HOW to Learn & Think

Maps — Mind — lots!

Memory
Reading
Selling — topics — BOOKS
Study
Aging
Genius

PRODUCTS

BUZAN'S BrainFriendly Courses & Products

audio
video — TAPES

management — life
posters — OTHER
kits

Maps — Mind — SOFTWARE

SEMINARS

TOPICS — creativity

management — life / change / knowledge

learning
communication

FOR — company — in-whole

trainers

open — public / business

education

CHARITY

#1001012

BRAIN — TRUST

research — use / apply / share

The Buzan Centres global network is ready to help you develop your Intellectual Capital Contact us today!

BUZAN CENTRES LTD
TEL: +44 (0) 1202 674676
FAX: +44 (0) 1202 674776
EMAIL: buzan@Mind-Map.com
www.Mind-Map.com

BUZAN CENTRES LTD

Learning & Thinking for the C21st

We are dedicated to creating a World where people know how to learn and think

MAKE THE MOST OF YOUR MIND

With customised solutions to enhance personal and professional performance and increase your Intellectual Capital

In-Company training
Licensing for companies and independant trainers
'Open' Business and Public Seminars
Educational Seminars

We are the only organisation that can license use of the Mind Maps® and associated trademarks

FOR FULL DETAILS OF
BUZAN LEARNING SEMINARS

and information on our range of BrainFriendly products including
- books
- software
- audio and video tapes
- support materials

SEND FOR OUR BROCHURE

Contact us at:

Email: **Buzan@Mind-Map.com**
Website: **www.Mind-Map.com**

Buzan Centres Ltd (Rest of World)
54 Parkstone Road
Poole, Dorset, BH15 2PG
Telephone: 44 (0) 1202 674676
Fax: 44 (0) 1202 674776

Buzan Centres Inc (Americas)
PO Box 4, Palm Beach
Florida, 33480, USA
Telephone: 001 561 881 0188
Fax: 001 561 434 1682

The Brain Trust Charity, #1001012 –

invites your contribution to assist brain research into effective processes for the enhancement of learning, thinking and the potential of all.